# PITTSBURGH

## STEELERS

PAT RYAN

CREATIVE ● EDUCATION INC.

01032 5453

Published by Creative Education, Inc.
123 S. Broad Street, Mankato, Minnesota 56001

Designed by Rita Marshall
Cover illustration by Lance Hidy Associates
Photos by Allsport, Photos by Sissac, Spectra-Action,
Sportschrome and Wide World Photos.

**Library of Congress Cataloging-in-Publication Data**

Ryan, Pat.
   Pittsburgh Steelers/Pat Ryan.
   p.   cm.
   ISBN 0-88682-380-3
   1.  Pittsburgh Steelers (Football team)—History.   I.  Title.
GV956.P57R93   1990
796.332′64′0974886—dc20                           90-41205
                                                                          CIP

In the early 1970s Pittsburgh, Pennsylvania, went through a renaissance, or rebirth. The change came because the people of Pittsburgh knew they had to rally to save their way of life. Work was slowing down at the steel mills and unemployment was high, but the people of Pittsburgh believed there was more to their town than mills, buildings, and smoke. They knew their best product was people.

The citizens went to work. The city of smoke was soon transformed into one of the finest cities in the United States. Since then Pittsburgh has been consistently on

*An early Pittsburgh star, John Henry Johnson*

many of the top-ten lists for cities with the highest quality of life. The Pittsburgh Steelers, the city's football team, experienced a rebirth of their own in the seventies.

The Steelers football club joined in the good fortune of Pittsburgh. With hard work it put together one of the finest football teams to ever play the game. The old-timers, however, would tell you that the Steelers weren't always winners.

1 9 3 3

*Art Rooney bought the original franchise for $2,500 with money he won on a lucky bet at Saratoga race track.*

## ONE MAN'S DREAM

For many years the Steelers were like a sleeping volcano. Smoldering and steaming, they had the potential for greatness but had yet to erupt. Only one man knew it would someday explode. That man was the legendary Art Rooney.

Arthur Joseph Rooney was born in 1901, the eldest of nine children of Daniel and Margaret Rooney. Art's father owned a saloon just a few blocks from Exposition Park, home of baseball's Pittsburgh Pirates and today the site of Three Rivers Stadium.

As a boy, Art grew up surrounded by sports, and he loved to play football and baseball. The young Rooney and his friends used to watch the Pirates through the knotholes in the wooden fence of Exposition Park. Rooney dreamed of some day being on the other side of the fence.

Years later Rooney's dream came true when he signed a contract with baseball's Boston Red Sox. Tragically, though, Art hurt his arm, ending his hopes for a pro career. Still the young Irishman didn't give up; he was determined to make sport his life.

In 1931 Rooney's dream became a reality when he took

*An Art Rooney favorite, L. C. Greenwood (#68).*

1 9 4 1

*Poor Pittsburgh! The Steelers lost a game to Green Bay by 47 points—their worst loss ever.*

on the challenge of putting a team on the field in the National Football League. The team was called the Pittsburgh Pirates, after his favorite baseball team, and though he expected it would be difficult, Art knew the people of Pittsburgh loved their football.

Years before Rooney fielded his team, Pennsylvania had established itself as the birthplace of professional football. In 1892 Pudge Hefelfinger was paid $500 to play for the Allegheny Athletic Association. Pudge earned his money by causing a fumble and carrying the football across the line and touching the ball to the ground for a four-point "touchdown." The Allegheny Athletic Association beat the Pittsburgh Athletic Club 4-0 in our nation's first professional football game.

In those initial days of football, the game resembled English rugby. In fact, the word touchdown was borrowed from the game of rugby. In that sport, the ball must touch the ground in the end zone. It didn't take long, however, for the players to adapt the event into a truly American game.

The first teams to play in the pro leagues were operated in the steel belts of Pennsylvania and were sponsored by local steel companies. The early clubs were like big families: they played together, worked together, and shared concern for each other. It was in this atmosphere of family football that the Pirates were born.

The volcano in Pittsburgh was in a dead sleep from the very beginning—asleep and having nightmares. The first nightmare came with the selection of the uniforms. Mr. Rooney clad his players in striped jerseys that made them look like fugitives from a chain gang. The opposing players called them "jailbirds." The team's play was as criminal as their uniforms; their record in that first year was 2-10. Rooney quickly got rid of the uniforms.

But Rooney had other problems, too. In 1938 the team was coached by a maverick, Johnny Blood. Usually the coaches worry about the players, but with Johnny the players had to keep track of the coach.

After losing a game in Los Angeles, Blood missed the train. When he failed to show up for practice, the team grew concerned, although not alarmed. After all in his short two-year career Blood was able to win only six of twenty-five games.

The following Sunday, Blood was finally spotted. He was at Wrigley Field watching the Packers play the Bears. When sportswriters asked him why he wasn't with his team, he explained, "Oh, we're not playing this week." No sooner did he get those words out of his mouth than the public-address announcer gave a final score: Philadelphia 14, Pittsburgh 7.

In 1940, in an attempt to end nine years of frustration, Rooney changed his team's name to the Steelers, a nickname that would represent the city's heritage. But the name change did not drastically alter the team's losing ways. A 7-4 record in 1942, under head coach Walt Kiesling, however, marked a big improvement. The Steeler's first winning season was due in part to the league-leading rushing of Bill Dudley. Unfortunately, the following year Dudley and a number of other star players joined the army to serve in World War II.

**1 9 5 2**

*Giant collapse! The Steelers defeated New York by 56 points—their biggest margin of victory ever.*

*A special teams' standout Rich Erenberg (#24), (pages 10–11).*

9

1 9 5 5

*Jim Finks threw a league-high 26 interceptions, which convinced him that it was time to retire.*

**W**alt Kiesling had three stints as coach of the Steelers, but not all of his years were as successful as 1942. His last term, in particular, was disastrous for Pittsburgh. In 1955 he released a young quarterback by the name of Johnny Unitas without giving him a minute of playing time. Kiesling told Rooney, "Unitas can't remember the plays. He's too dumb." Yet the Baltimore Colts decided to give Unitas a chance. Unitas, in return, led the Colts to three championships and was named by one group of sports-writers as the greatest quarterback in the history of the NFL. After mistakes like this, the Steelers' luck just had to change.

In 1957 it finally did, beginning with the naming of Buddy Parker as their new coach. Parker's first decision got the Steelers rolling. He put flamboyant Bobby Layne at quarterback and the Steelers were winners at last. Parker also had John Henry Johnson in the backfield, crushing tacklers on his way to the Hall of Fame. And on defense he had Gene "Big Daddy" Lipscomb, who was a one-man wrecking crew.

The Steelers, with these stars leading the way, had five non-losing records in eight years. In Layne's last season with the team, 1962, the team finished 9-5 to earn a post-season birth. The volcano was shaking. Their hopes were quickly dashed, however, with a loss to Detroit 17 to 10, but the rumblings would continue.

Art Rooney could sense something was stirring, and he responded by going to a winning program to find his next coach. The powerhouse team in Baltimore had an assistant coach by the name of Chuck Noll who wanted a chance to lead. In 1969 Rooney signed the Steelers fourteenth head coach, Chuck Noll. Charles Henry Noll, in a few short years, would take the Steelers from doormat to dynasty.

Ironically, Noll was patient. He wanted to use the college draft to build the team rather than bring in aging veterans. He was also committed to defense. In 1969 Noll used his number one pick to sign Joe Greene from North Texas State. Greene would be the first in what was to be the most successful string of selections in the history of pro football. In that first year, Noll also signed offensive great Jon Kolb from Oklahoma State and defensive standout L.C. Greenwood from Arkansas AM & N. But it was the 1970 draft that really began to change things for the Steelers.

1 9 6 2

*John Henry Johnson became the first Steeler to rush for 1,000 yards in a single season.*

At the end of the 1969 season, the Steelers and the Bears had tied for the worst record in the NFL. A coin toss would decide which team would have the number one draft pick. As the coin sailed into the air everything seemed to be in slow motion. The Steelers called "heads." As the coin fell to the floor, Rooney and Noll held their breaths in anticipation. Seconds later, NFL commissioner Pete Rozelle announced that the coin had come up heads. The first pick belonged to Pittsburgh.

This big moment in Steeler history occurred in New Orleans and Noll and Rooney remained in the South to select the nation's premier college quarterback, Louisiana Tech's, Terry Bradshaw.

The young quarterback was as unlikely a star as the Steelers were winners. Terry was born September 2, 1948, in Shreveport, Louisiana. He was the second of Bill and Novice Bradshaw's three sons.

In the Deep South, football is the number one sport,

and like most youngsters Terry began playing the game at an early age. But unlike many future stars, Terry had to prove himself from the very beginning. Many coaches thought he was too skinny to play football. When Terry was in junior high school, he was even cut from the team. He was so upset that he cried when he got home from practice. "Your time will come," his father told him. "Just make sure that you're ready when it does."

Bradshaw's opportunity came as a senior in high school, and he was indeed ready. In his first season as a starting quarterback he completed 47 percent of his passes for 1,400 yards and twenty-one touchdowns. Terry was getting a lot of attention by major colleges, but strangely enough not because of his ability to throw a football. Rather, it was his ability to throw a javelin.

Terry had taken up the javelin in order to have a spring sport. His arm was so strong that by twelfth grade he was the best high school javelin thrower in the country. In fact, Terry set the national high school record of 244 feet 11 inches. Over 200 colleges offered him scholarships to throw the javelin. Terry turned them all down, however, because he wanted to play college football.

One of the few football offers he got was from Louisiana State, but he wanted to have the opportunity to play as a freshman; so instead, Terry chose a small college only seventy-five miles from his home, Louisiana Tech.

Four years later, by the time he graduated, the skinny boy who was too small for the junior high team had grown into a muscular six-feet three-inch, 215-pound man. Bradshaw was quick, too. He could run the forty-yard dash in 4.6 seconds. The pro scouts were licking their chops.

When Terry reported to the Steelers' rookie camp, he

*A defensive teammate of Bradshaw's, Jack Ham (#59).*

felt as awkward as he had back in junior high. Professional football was going to be a big adjustment for him. Terry knew he had the physical skills, but he was scared.

1 9 7 0

*Quarterback Terry Bradshaw was the first player selected overall in the college draft.*

Terry's first game as a pro must have reminded him of being in junior high as well. Nothing seemed to work. He had tried to make the game a memorable one, but by the end of the contest the Steelers' fans thought they had been sold some rotten goods. Bradshaw's passes looked like wounded ducks as they wobbled into the hands of the joyful Houston Oilers.

In all, Bradshaw misfired on nine straight passes and was only four for sixteen when Noll finally benched him. After the game Bradshaw told reporters, "The benching put a big lump in my throat. I told myself, 'What now, big shot? Everybody was counting on you and you blew it. You better hide when you get to that locker room.'"

Despite the poor start, Bradshaw bounced back. In his mind Terry could hear the encouraging words of his father from years past, "You better be ready." It was a matter of confidence, Bradshaw would admit years later. "The worst thing was I lost my confidence," he reflected. "Totally. What's the worst thing that can happen to a quarterback? He loses his confidence." Finally, Bradshaw got so desperate he had his old college coach send him the films from his college games so he could see who he was. "I was trying to be Joe Namath or anybody, instead of being myself," he reflected. Terry Bradshaw at last found himself.

## THE TEAM OF THE SEVENTIES

While the Pittsburgh quarterback was working through his problems, the Pittsburgh offensive line was beginning to gel. It was fortunate because Noll knew that he had to buy more time for his young quarterback. The opposition would eat up an offense that could only pass. Noll needed to balance the offensive attack with a strong running game.

In the meantime Noll continued to hit the college draft for bigger, faster, and better players. In 1970 and 1971 he was able to sign Mel Blount, Frank Lewis, John McKin, and Joe Gilliam. Position by position, Noll was building a structure of steel, but one beam was still missing.

1 9 7 2

*He's great! Rookie of the Year Franco Harris rushed for 1,055 yards and scored eleven touchdowns!*

Noll found his last pillar of strength in his own backyard. The other game in Pennsylvania was up the road a piece at Penn State. There, coach Joe Paterno had a young running back named Franco Harris who was ripping through college lines. In a short time, he would become the final support for the beginning of the "Steel Age."

Mean Joe Green, who some have called the most loyal Steeler of them all, said of Harris, "Franco was the key man on our ball club. We were coming on every year, getting better and better. All we needed was the catalyst and Franco was it."

In 1972 Franco, like Terry Bradshaw, got a slow start as a rookie. In his first game, Harris gained only thirty-five yards and fumbled twice in a loss to Cincinnati. Backfield coach Dick Hoak later admitted, "We thought we had a real dud on our hands." Midway through his rookie season, however, Harris got on track. He rushed for over 100 yards in six straight games, equaling Jim Brown's NFL record. Boosted by Harris's fine performance, the Steelers won nine of their next ten games en route to their first play-off berth since 1962.

Great players make great plays, and never was this more

*Franco Harris's running mate, (#20) Rocky Bleier, (pages 18–19).*

*Wow! Franco Harris's single season rushing total was 1,246 yards— the most ever by any Pittsburgh player.*

true than in Pittsburgh's first play-off game. The Steelers were up against John Madden's Oakland Raiders and were trailing 7-6 with only twenty-two seconds left in the game. Bradshaw had only one play left; he licked his fingers and called, "66 option." In the Raider defensive huddle, the man they called "the Assassin," Jack Tatum, said, "One more time."

From his own forty-yard line, Bradshaw rolled right, planted his foot, and threw for running back John Fuqua. Just as the ball arrived, Tatum hit Fuqua with a ferocious blow, and the ball flew fifteen yards backward. Running back Franco Harris, who was following the play, plucked the ball out of the air as it was barely off his shoe tops and rambled sixty yards for the winning touchdown.

Harris's reception was made possible by his extra effort. He was supposed to block for Bradshaw, but when he saw his quarterback scramble to the right he decided to drift downfield. "I thought I could be another target for Terry," reflected Harris, "or help block for whoever caught the pass. I was just fortunate to be in the right place."

The scoreboard flashed Merry Christmas, and the fans got their gift. Forty years was a long time to wait, but the volcano was finally bubbling. The Miami Dolphins would halt the Steeler activity momentarily with their 21-17 victory in the AFC championship game, but everyone knew that Franco's "Immaculate Reception" was a sign of good things to come.

Noll's draft-pick success continued to roll in 1974. In a draft that former 49er coach Bill Walsh would call "maybe the best draft ever," the Steelers, in five rounds, selected Lynn Swann, Jack Lambert, John Stallworth, and Mike Webster; which would eventually translate into twenty-four Pro Bowl appearances, sixteen Super Bowl rings, and four potential Hall of Famers. What a draft!

Propelled by the success of the draft, Art Rooney's Black and Gold found themselves in the Super Bowl the next year, and they were not going to let forty-one years of waiting keep them from crossing the final goal line.

Led by their offensive line of Clack, Mullins, and Webster Pittsburgh blew their opponents, the Minnesota Vikings, off the line in Super Bowl IX. Franco Harris followed them for 158 yards rushing, as the Steelers beat the Vikings 16-6.

"Today's win made all the other years worth it," said Rooney, his voice quivering with emotion. "I am happy for the coaches and players, but I'm especially happy for the Pittsburgh fans. They deserved this." The volcano had finally erupted.

The Steelers didn't want to be known as one-year wonders, so this dedicated team of immense talent went back to work. "Two for two" became the battle cry. No one expected the Steelers to repeat. Only two teams had ever done it—the Green Bay Packers and the Miami Dolphins.

During the 1975 season, the Steelers won eleven consecutive games to finish 12-2. In the play-offs they defeated Baltimore 28-10 and Oakland 16-10. Pittsburgh was once again headed for the Super Bowl. Their opponent this time were the Dallas Cowboys.

In the big game Bradshaw, Harris, and Lynn Swann put on another powerful offensive display. At the same time the defense kept Roger Staubach bottled up, and in the end they beat the Cowboys 21-17. With the victory Chuck

1 9 7 7

*On October 9, John Stallworth began the first of 67 consecutive games in which he caught a pass.*

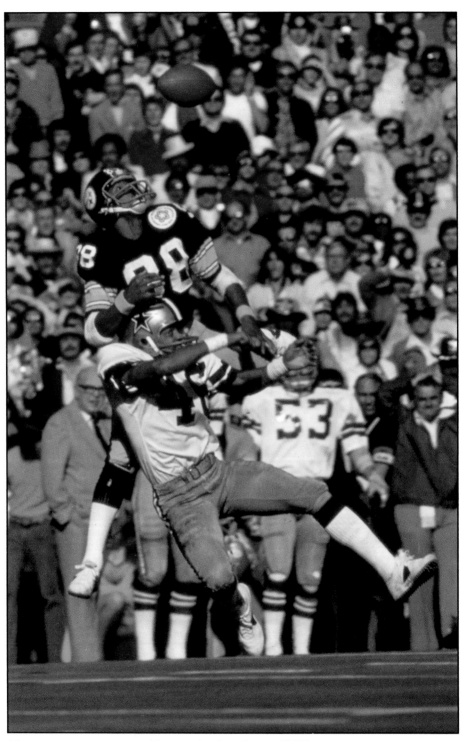

*The amazing Lynn Swann (#88).*

Noll joined Vince Lombardi and Don Shula as the only coaches to win consecutive Super Bowls. Everyone now wondered could they make possibly it three?

Unfortunately for Pittsburgh fans the answer was no. In what has been called the Steelers' "years of distraction" the team lost in the play-offs in 1976 and 1977. In an attempt to turn things around, Noll changed his game plans for 1978 and 1979. The first two Super Bowls came on the ground; if the Steelers were going to win again, Noll realized it would have to be in the air.

Coach Noll and Bradshaw were going to open up the offense, and John Stallworth and Lynn Swann would be the key players in the next assault. Their plan worked: the Steelers finished the 1978 season with a 14-2 record, the best in the NFL.

With his team rejuvenated Terry Bradshaw was once again in the spotlight as he led the Steelers into their third Super Bowl. This time Bradshaw would play the best game of his life. He passed for 318 yards and four touchdowns, and became the first quarterback ever to win three Super Bowls.

One year later, Bradshaw found himself on the same stage with the same cast of supporting actors. Super Bowl XIV called for a special game plan, though, against the tough pass defense of the L.A. Rams. Bradshaw and his receivers knew that L.A. was expecting the short pass, so Bradshaw and his wide-outs put the "hook-and-go" pattern into the offense. Stallworth and Swann would fake a hook back toward the line to draw defenders in, then whirl and fly deep.

In the fourth quarter trailing 19-17, the Steelers had the

1 9 8 2

*From 1974–82, Lynn Swann's graceful, acrobatic receptions resulted in 5,462 yards and 51 touchdowns.*

*Clockwise: Louis Lipps, Bubby Brister, Franco Harris, Jack Lambert.*

ball on their own twenty-seven-yard line. Bradshaw decided it was time to go deep. Stallworth hooked and sprinted downfield. As Stallworth turned back, he saw the perfect spiral outlined by the blue sky, he hauled it in, and dashed in for the seventy-three-yard score. The Steelers went up 24-19.

A few minutes later, Bradshaw iced the game when he threw another bomb, this time for forty-five yards. On the strength of their Louisiana quarterback's arm the Steelers proudly entered the soft glow of football history with a historic fourth Super Bowl championship.

1 9 8 3

*Jack Lambert became the only linebacker in history to be named to the Pro Bowl for nine straight years.*

Were the Steelers of the seventies the greatest team in professional football history? Many argue that that honor should be bestowed upon the 49ers, the Dolphins, or the Packers. Other experts believe the Steelers were the best because they had a great offense but an even greater defense.

The "Steel Curtain" of Greene, Dwight "Mad Dog" White, Ernie Holmes, and L.C. Greenwood dominated the trenches. As a result, the opposing teams' quarterbacks spent most of the time on their backs.

As the Steelers entered the eighties, the greats retired one by one. Chuck Noll tried to rebuild his dynasty by drafting his way back into contention. Under this philosophy the Steelers managed to go three more years without a losing season. And by 1984, the Steelers had captured the American Football Conference's Central Division title for the ninth time in thirteen seasons.

In the play-offs the Steelers came back with the new and the old. With veterans Jack Lambert, John Stallworth and Donnie Snell joining the "new Steelers," quarterback

*Running back Merril Hoge, (pages 26–27).*

Mark Malone and receiver Louis Lipps, Pittsburgh beat the Broncos and went into the championship game against the Dolphins.

The new Steelers, however, came up short, but the 45-28 loss didn't worry Art Rooney. "This is an upbeat team," he said. "There is so much youth, so much hope for the future."

1 9 8 8

*In his twentieth season as head coach of the Steelers, Chuck Noll's record was 5-11.*

---

## A RETURN TO SUCCESS

Unfortunately, the Steelers' good fortunes did not continue. The next three seasons they suffered through many losses. By 1988 there were rumblings in Pittsburgh, but not from the Steelers. A few fans and writers were calling for coach Noll's dismissal. But Art Rooney knew that Noll could win with the right talent. Noll and his staff agreed with Art. They knew the team needed a general, a leader, a fierce competitor. To find one the coaching staff would once again head to Louisiana. This time they would find a signal caller with a rather unusual handle, Bubby.

Walter Andrew Brister III got his nickname "Bubby" from his five older sisters back in Monroe, Louisiana. Bubby, like many other top quarterbacks, was also a star in baseball. He was drafted by the Detroit Tigers in 1981 and even played a few years in the minor leagues. Bubby, however, eventually went back to his first love, football and enrolled at Northeast Louisiana.

At Northeast Louisiana, Bubby threw for seventeen touchdowns and 2,280 yards in his senior year. The Steelers drafted him in the third round in 1986, but it took Brister a few years to work his way into a starting position.

In 1988 Bubby finally got his chance. In a splendid performance against Houston, Brister gave the Oilers their only home loss when he came in and spearheaded a 37-34 upset. Bubby tossed three touchdown passes. Two of them went to Louis Lipps. Brister connected with Lipps for touchdowns of eighty and sixty-five yards. Late in the game Bubby marched the team eighty yards in eight plays, capping off the drive with a sixteen-yard toss to Merrill Hoge with twenty seconds remaining. For his efforts Bubby was named offensive player of the week.

1 9 8 9

*Pittsburgh wide receiver Louis Lipps caught fifty passes for nearly 1000 yards.*

Despite the loss, Houston head coach Jerry Glanville liked what he saw in Brister. "We put some hellacious hits on the kid and he kept ticking," he remarked. "You can't bother him with physical abuse. This guy is a competitor. If he wasn't starting at quarterback, he'd be starting at free safety and punching people in the mouth."

From this performance Brister's confidence grew and grew. At the spring minicamp in 1989, Bubby walked into the locker room, grabbed a piece of chalk, and wrote "PLAY-OFFS 89" on the blackboard. In the first two games of the campaign, however, the Steelers were outscored 92-10. Brister gave another pep talk.

"I say whatever I think needs to be said," Brister remarked. "We need leadership on this team. It's my job to keep everybody jacked up and ready to play." The talk worked. Nine months after Bubby made his blackboard prediction, the Steelers were back in Houston, this time for the play-offs.

After sixty minutes of football were almost up, the Black and Gold were losing. Bubby and the offense had one more chance. Brister led the Steelers down the field in a

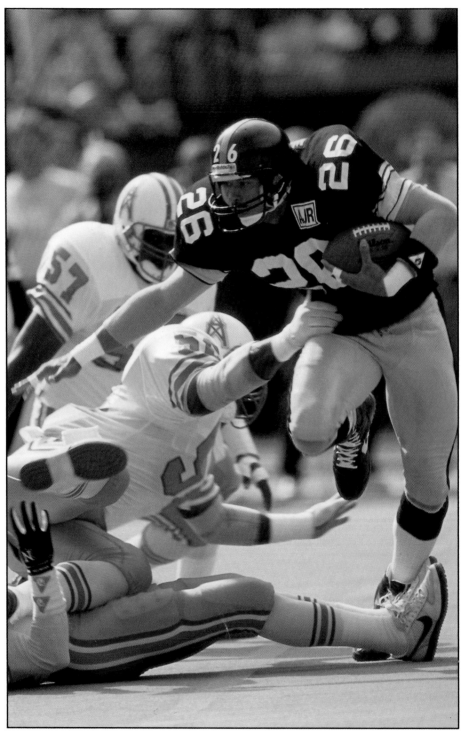

*Cornerback and return specialist Rod Woodson.*

*Running back Tim Worley.*

*Quarterback Bubby Brister emerged as a team leader as the Steelers entered the new decade.*

last gasp effort. Time was running out. He took the Steelers eighty-two yards in eleven plays. With only seconds remaining, he handed off to Merrill Hoge for the score. Bayou Bubby was in overtime in the play-offs!

All the defense had to do was give Steeler kicker Gary Anderson a chance to win it in overtime. When he got his chance Anderson's size 6½ right shoe met the ball square and it sailed fifty yards for the game winner.

The storybook season would finally come to an end the next week in Denver, but the fans knew that it was really only chapter one in a new book called *Bubby Ball.* Brister's predictions alone, however, won't win games. It will take talent and teamwork. Rod Woodson, Tim Worley, and Dwayne Woodruff are the players of the future for the Steelers. If Brister falters he has a fine supporting cast.

In the nineties Brister's teammates will anxiously await Bubby's next prediction. Who knows, the tough, cocky, quarterback might walk up to the chalkboard next time and write "SUPER BOWL!"

If so it will continue the proud tradition Art Rooney began more than fifty years ago. And although Rooney, who died before the beginning of the 1989 season, didn't get a chance to tell Chuck Noll, he knew the Steelers would be back. The kid who used to hang around the ballpark was gone, but his spirit and love for the game will always be a part of the Pittsburgh Steelers.